Written by
Ray Miller, Vivian Fernandez, and Karen Price
Illustrated by Dan Jankowski

References
The World Book Encyclopedia © 1993 World Book, Inc.
U.S. Census Bureau, 1990 census results released 1996

© 1999 by Pace Products, Inc.
333 Semoran Commerce Place, Apopka, FL 32703

Printed in Canada
ISBN 1-58295-034-2

Celebrating the 50 States!

If you open an American history book, you can find out about everything from the Revolutionary War to the Apollo moon missions. Flip through a United States geography book and you'll see amazing pictures of the Grand Canyon and the Statue of Liberty. Now, there's another way to explore the rich history, tradition, and geography of the United States. Just pick up a quarter and look at the "tails" side!

On December 1, 1997, President Clinton signed the "50 State Quarters™ Program Act." This act allows the Department of the Treasury to issue a series of new quarters honoring the 50 states. From 1999 to 2008, five state quarters will be issued each year in the order the states became part of the United States of America.

Starting with Delaware and ending with Hawaii, each special-edition quarter will feature a design unique to its state. You never know what picture will be on your quarters. You might find George Washington crossing the Delaware River, or Connecticut's majestic Charter Oak tree. The 50 States Quarter Program will definitely have you taking a closer look at your change.

Starting a 50 States Quarters Collection

These quarters make an impressive addition to any coin collection. For people who don't already have a coin collection, these quarters are the perfect starting point!

You can keep your quarters in the folder included in this kit. To add a quarter to your collection, put the quarter in the circular slot and press. The quarter will stay in place.

"Changing" History

Although the 50 State Quarters Program will change the appearance of the quarter, it isn't the first time the coin has received a new look. From the late 18th century to the early 20th century, the quarter featured the same two symbols. The front pictured Lady Liberty, but her position, hair, and dress have changed from time to time. The back pictured our national bird, the bald eagle. It, too, changed in appearance over time. The eagle started out as small bird, which many people thought looked like a pigeon. Eventually, the eagle design was changed to reflect a strong and proud image.

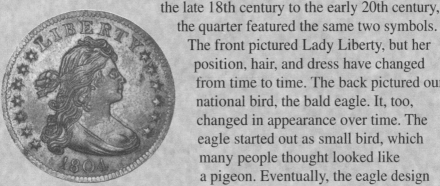

**Front of 1804
Lady Liberty Quarter**

To celebrate the *bicentennial* (200-year anniversary) of George Washington's birthday, in 1932 a silhouette of Washington's head replaced Lady Liberty on the front of the quarter. It has appeared there ever since. In 1976, the United States celebrated the bicentennial of the signing of the Declaration of Independence. That event marked a temporary change in the quarter's appearance. In 1975 and 1976, a colonial drummer replaced the eagle. From 1977 to 1999, the quarter's design remained the same.

**Back of 1975–76
Bicentennial Quarter**

Another Change

With the 50 State Quarters Program, the quarter will go through the biggest design changes in history. The eagle emblem on the back of the quarter will be replaced with designs representing each state. To make as much room as possible, the words "United States of America" and "Quarter Dollar" are being moved from the back of the coin to the front. Look at the illustrations below to compare the old and new designs.

Old Quarter—Front

Old Quarter—Back

New Quarter—Front

New Quarter—Back

Design Your State's Quarter!

The best part about the 50 State Quarters Program is that anyone can submit a design for approval. That means you can try designing the back of your state's quarter.* Use the guide on the opposite page to draw your own design. If you don't want to ruin the page by cutting it, trace the guide on blank paper.

*Some of the state quarters designs have already been selected. To find out if your state's quarter has been designed, contact your governor's office or log on to the United States Mint website at *www.usmint.gov/50states*. You can find out much more about the 50 State Quarters Program there.

Before you begin your design, read these important guidelines.

- Designs may include state landmarks (natural and man-made), landscapes, historic buildings, symbols of state resources or industries, official flowers and trees, state images (such as a cactus for Arizona or a bronco for Wyoming), and state outlines.
- Your design should appeal to all citizens of the state. Do not include subjects or symbols that may offend anyone.
- Do not use state flags, state seals, and words or phrases in your design.
- Do not include a head-and-shoulders portrait of any person, living or dead, or any portrait of a living person in your design.

You must submit your design idea to your state governor's office. The governor will select at least three and no more than five designs. The governor will then send the designs to the United States Mint. There, the approved design concepts will be drawn by artists and returned to the governor, who will choose one of those designs.

Leave this area blank.

Leave this area blank.

Alabama
"The Heart of Dixie"

Capital
Montgomery

State Bird
Yellowhammer

State Flower
Camellia

Land Area
50,750 sq. mi.
(131,443 sq. km)

State Tree
Southern pine

Rank in Size
28th

Before becoming a state in 1819, **Alabama** belonged to France, then Great Britain, then Spain. In 1795, the Treaty of San Lorenzo, signed by the United States and Spain, gave the area to the United States. It was then called the Mississippi Territory. The Creek Indian tribe fought the United States government for its rights to the land, but surrendered in 1814 after several defeats. In 1817, the area was known as the Alabama Territory. The territory became the 22nd state in 1819.

 Statehood Year: 1819
The 22nd state
Coin Issue Year: 2003

Alaska
"The Last Frontier"

Capital
Juneau

State Bird
Willow ptarmigan

State Flower
Forget-me-not

Land Area
570,374 sq. mi.
(1,477,268 sq. km)

State Tree
Sitka spruce

Rank in Size
1st

The United States bought **Alaska** from Russia in 1867. At first, many Americans thought the purchase was foolish. Then, in 1880 and again in 1896, gold was discovered in Alaska. This discovery brought thousands of people to the state. In 1942, the Japanese occupied two Alaskan islands during World War II. That same year the United States government built a military supply road to Alaska, called the Alaska Highway. This highway allowed people to move more freely from the lower 48 states to Alaska. After the war, many Americans agreed that Alaska should be given statehood. This was finally accomplished in 1959.

Statehood Year: 1959
The 49th state
Coin Issue Year: 2008

Arizona
"The Grand Canyon State"

Capital
Phoenix

State Bird
Cactus wren

State Flower
Saguaro
(giant cactus)

Land Area
113,642 sq. mi.
(294,333 sq. km)

State Tree
Paloverde

Rank in Size
6th

In the 1800s, **Arizona** was an exciting, dangerous place to live. One reason was that settlers always feared Indian attacks. In 1864, Kit Carson led a campaign that resulted in the defeat of the Navajo tribe, but the Apache were a threat until their leader, Geronimo, surrendered in 1886. Even so, many people came to Arizona to mine its gold, silver, and copper deposits. Boom towns such as Tombstone sprung up around the mines. In 1890, many in the state voiced their desire for statehood. But the United States government's disagreement with some articles in the state's constitution held things up, and Arizona did not become a state until 1912.

 Statehood Year: 1912
The 48th state
Coin Issue Year: 2008

Arkansas
"The Land of Opportunity"

Capital
Little Rock

State Bird
Mockingbird

State Flower
Apple blossom

Land Area
52,075 sq. mi.
(134,875 sq. km)

State Tree
Pine tree

Rank in Size
27th

In 1812, **Arkansas** was part of the Missouri Territory. In 1819, the United States government changed the area's name to the Arkansaw Territory. When Arkansas became a state in 1836, the issue of slavery was being debated in the South. In 1861, after the start of the Civil War, Arkansas *seceded* (withdrew) from the Union to support the Confederacy (the states that wanted to keep slavery). In 1868, after the war ended, Arkansas was readmitted into the Union.

 Statehood Year: 1836
The 25th state
Coin Issue Year: 2003

California
"The Golden State"

Capital
Sacramento

State Bird
California quail

State Flower
Golden poppy

Land Area
155,973 sq. mi.
(403,971 sq. km)

State Tree
California
redwood

Rank in Size
3rd

California became a province of Mexico in 1822, right after Mexico won independence from Spain. In 1841, settlers from the East formed wagon trains and crossed the country to settle in California. These settlers wanted California to become part of the United States, but Mexico did not want to sell its territory. After a two-year war, Mexico surrendered to California in 1848. California became a state in 1850, just two years after gold was discovered there and thousands of people flocked to the state to make their fortunes.

 Statehood Year: 1850
The 31st state
Coin Issue Year: 2005

Colorado
"The Centennial State"

Capital
Denver

State Bird
Lark bunting

State Flower
Rocky Mountain
columbine

Land Area
103,729 sq. mi.
(268,658 sq. km)

State Tree
Colorado
blue spruce

Rank in Size
8th

When gold was discovered in **Colorado** in 1858, nearly 100,000 people rushed to the region. Many went back home after failing to find gold. Those who stayed called the area the Jefferson Territory. The United States Congress refused to recognize this territory, and in 1861 set up its own Colorado Territory, which had the same boundaries as the present-day state. During the early days of this territory, troops battled Cheyenne, Arapaho, and Ute Indians. In 1870, the railroad joined Colorado to the East, and more people came to the territory. In 1876, Colorado achieved statehood.

 Statehood Year: 1876
The 38th state
Coin Issue Year: 2006

Connecticut
"The Constitution State"

Capital
Hartford

State Bird
American robin

State Flower
Mountain laurel

Land Area
4,845 sq. mi.
(12,550 sq. km)

State Tree
White oak

Rank in Size
48th

Connecticut was settled by English colonists from Massachusetts in 1633. In 1662, the king of England gave the Connecticut Colony a *charter* (similar to a contract) granting the colony a strip of land bordered by a Connecticut bay on one side and the Pacific Ocean on the other. Neither the king nor the colonists realized that the Pacific Ocean was thousands of miles away! In 1665, the Connecticut Colony became larger when it joined the New Haven Colony. The colony supported independence from Great Britain and sent hundreds of men to fight in the Revolutionary War. Connecticut became one of the original 13 United States colonies in 1788.

 Statehood Year: 1788
The 5th state
Coin Issue Year: 1999

Delaware
"The First State"

Capital
Dover

State Bird
Blue hen chicken

State Flower
Peach blossom

Land Area
1,955 sq. mi.
(5,063 sq. km)

State Tree
American holly

Rank in Size
49th

Delaware was first settled in 1631 by the Dutch. But by 1632, all the settlers had been killed by Indians. In 1638, Swedish colonists settled in the region and called the territory New Sweden. In 1664, the British took over. They gave the land to William Penn to add to his colony of Pennsylvania. But by 1701, the area became a separate region called the Three Lower Colonies. It was not called Delaware until 1776, after Lord De La Warr, the first governor of the Virginia colony. Delaware was the first state to approve the United States Constitution.

 Statehood Year: 1787
The 1st state
Coin Issue Year: 1999

Florida
"The Sunshine State"

Capital
Tallahassee

State Bird
Mockingbird

State Flower
Orange blossom

Land Area
53,997 sq. mi.
(139,853 sq. km)

State Tree
Sabal palm

Rank in Size
26th

In 1513, Spanish explorer Juan Ponce de León arrived in **Florida**. He thought Florida was an island and claimed it for Spain. The king of Spain ordered him to colonize the land. When he tried to do so in 1521, he and his men were attacked by Indians, and Ponce de León was wounded by an arrow. With other survivors, he sailed to Cuba, where he died. The French came to settle in 1564, but were driven out by the Spanish in 1565. For most of the next 200 years, Spain ruled the Florida region. In 1819, Spain gave Florida to the United States. Florida was admitted to the Union in 1845.

 Statehood Year: 1845
The 27th state
Coin Issue Year: 2004

Georgia
"The Empire State of the South"

Capital
Atlanta

State Bird
Brown thrasher

State Flower
Cherokee rose

Land Area
57,919 sq. mi.
(150,010 sq. km)

State Tree
Live oak

Rank in Size
21st

In the 1500s, the Spanish claimed the southeastern United States, including Florida and **Georgia**. But in 1564, the French set up a colony in Florida. Spain fought and defeated France for control of the land. Then, ignoring the claims of Spain, the British settled near Savannah in 1733. They fought Spain over the Florida-Georgia boundary in 1739. The British lost that battle, but fought the Spanish again in 1742 and won control of Georgia. In 1754, Georgia became a royal province, governed by England's King George. When the American Revolution broke out, most Georgians fought for independence. After the war, Georgia approved the United States Constitution and became the fourth state admitted to the Union.

 Statehood Year: 1788
The 4th state
Coin Issue Year: 1999

Hawaii
"The Aloha State"

Capital Honolulu	**State Bird** Hawaiian goose
State Flower Yellow hibiscus	**Land Area** 6,423 sq. mi. (16,637 sq. km)
State Tree Kukui	**Rank in Size** 47th

For many years, **Hawaii** was a monarchy (governed by a king or queen). But in 1893, a revolution removed the queen from office. In 1900, Hawaii was made a United States territory. Soon after, the United States Navy built a naval base in Pearl Harbor. That base was involved in a major event in United States history. On December 7, 1941, 33 Japanese ships and 360 airplanes attacked Pearl Harbor. About 3,700 people lost their lives. This event pulled the United States into World War II. During the war many Hawaiian citizens proved their loyalty to the United States, and in 1959 Hawaii became a state.

 Statehood Year: 1959
The 50th state
Coin Issue Year: 2008

Idaho
"The Gem State"

Capital Boise	**State Bird** Mountain bluebird
State Flower Syringa	**Land Area** 82,751 sq. mi. (214,325 sq. km)
State Tree Western white pine	**Rank in Size** 11th

The famous explorers Lewis and Clark traveled through **Idaho** in 1805. A few years later, a British fur trader moved into the area. He was soon followed by other traders. In 1860, a group of Mormons (a religious group) settled the first permanent town in Idaho, called Franklin. When gold was discovered in Orofino Creek that same year, people rushed to the region. In 1863, the Idaho Territory was organized. With the development of the railroad came more settlers. In 1890, Idaho became a state.

 Statehood Year: 1890
The 43rd state
Coin Issue Year: 2007

Illinois
"The Land of Lincoln"

Capital
Springfield

State Flower
Native violet

State Tree
White oak

State Bird
Cardinal

Land Area
55,593 sq. mi.
(143,987 sq. km)

Rank in Size
24th

French explorers Marquette and Jolliet are thought to be the first Europeans to travel through **Illinois**. Later, in 1699, French priests founded a mission in a fur-trading post. In 1717, Illinois became part of Louisiana, which was a French colony at the time. In 1763, after Great Britain's victory in the French and Indian War, the British owned the colony. After the Revolutionary War, Illinois became part of the Northwest Territory. In 1809, it was called the Illinois Territory, and in 1818, Illinois became a state.

 Statehood Year: 1818
The 21st state
Coin Issue Year: 2003

Indiana
"The Hoosier State"

Capital
Indianapolis

State Flower
Peony

State Tree
Tulip tree

State Bird
Cardinal

Land Area
35,870 sq. mi.
(92,904 sq. km)

Rank in Size
38th

Fur traders from France, then Great Britain, were the first *immigrants* (people who came from another country) to settle in **Indiana**. After the French were defeated in 1763, the British took over the fur trade in Indiana and surrounding areas. Indiana became part of the Northwest Territory after the Revolutionary War. In 1800, Congress established the Indiana Territory. At first, the territory had to contend with Indian forces, led by Tecumseh. But the Indians were defeated in 1811. In 1816, Indiana became the 19th state to join the Union.

 Statehood Year: 1816
The 19th state
Coin Issue Year: 2002

Iowa
"The Hawkeye State"

Capital Des Moines	**State Bird** Eastern goldfinch
State Flower Wild rose	**Land Area** 55,875 sq. mi. (144,716 sq. km)
State Tree Oak	**Rank in Size** 23rd

In 1831, the United States government wanted the Native Americans who lived in Illinois to move to **Iowa**. Chief Black Hawk refused to move. This led to the Black Hawk War of 1832. After the Native American tribes were defeated, they gave up a strip of land along the Mississippi River. Settlers quickly moved into this land, establishing the first permanent white settlements in Iowa. In 1838, the United States government created the Territory of Iowa. Iowa became a state in 1846.

 Statehood Year: 1846
The 29th state
Coin Issue Year: 2004

Kansas
"The Sunflower State"

Capital Topeka	**State Bird** Western meadowlark
State Flower Sunflower	**Land Area** 81,823 sq. mi. (211,922 sq. km)
State Tree Cottonwood	**Rank in Size** 13th

In 1825, the United States government gave the Indians land in **Kansas** in return for taking land from them in the East. About 30 Indian tribes settled in the region of Kansas. By 1850, more and more settlers wanted to live there, so the government took back much of the Indians' land. The Indians fought back, but eventually most of them were moved to Oklahoma. In 1854, Congress established the Territory of Kansas, and in 1861, Kansas became a state.

 Statehood Year: 1861
The 34th state
Coin Issue Year: 2005

Kentucky
"The Bluegrass State"

Capital
Frankfort

State Flower
Goldenrod

State Tree
Kentucky
coffeetree

State Bird
Kentucky cardinal

Land Area
39,732 sq. mi.
(102,907 sq. km)

Rank in Size
36th

In the 1700s, explorers, including Daniel Boone, traveled the hills of **Kentucky**. During their explorations, they often met up with Indians and were forced to turn back. In 1776, Kentucky became part of Virginia, and many people from that colony moved to Kentucky to settle. After a series of British-supported Indian attacks, the settlers cut off the supply of weapons the British gave to the Indians. The attacks slowed down, and the settlers gained control of the land. Soon, they drew up a constitution. In 1792, Kentucky became a state.

 Statehood Year: 1792
The 15th state
Coin Issue Year: 2001

Louisiana
"The Pelican State"

Capital
Baton Rouge

State Flower
Magnolia

State Tree
Bald cypress

State Bird
Brown pelican

Land Area
43,566 sq. mi.
(112,836 sq. km)

Rank in Size
33rd

Louisiana was once a French colony, named in honor of King Louis XIV of France. In 1803, France sold the territory to the United States for about $15 million as part of the Louisiana Purchase. This sale doubled the area of what was then the United States. At that time, Louisiana included parts of Montana, North Dakota, South Dakota, Iowa, Missouri, New Mexico, Colorado, Oklahoma, Minnesota, Nebraska, Kansas, and Arkansas. After the purchase, Congress divided the territory into smaller parts. What we now call Louisiana was known as the Territory of Orleans. In 1812, it was renamed Louisiana and became a state.

 Statehood Year: 1812
The 18th state
Coin Issue Year: 2002

Maine
"The Pine Tree State"

Capital
Augusta

State Bird
Chickadee

State Flower
White pine cone
and tassel

Land Area
30,865 sq. mi.
(79,939 sq. km)

State Tree
White pine

Rank in Size
39th

The first English colonists settled in **Maine** in 1607, 13 years before the Pilgrims landed in Massachusetts. But a harsh winter, lack of supplies, and conflicts with Native Americans forced the settlers back to England in 1608. In the 1620s, more English colonists arrived in Maine and established permanent settlements. In the mid-1600s, Maine was made part of the Massachusetts Bay Colony, and remained so until 1819, when the people of Maine voted for separation. One year later, Maine became a state.

 Statehood Year: 1820
The 23rd state
Coin Issue Year: 2003

Maryland
"The Old Line State"

Capital
Annapolis

State Bird
Baltimore oriole

State Flower
Black-eyed Susan

Land Area
9,775 sq. mi.
(25,316 sq. km)

State Tree
White oak

Rank in Size
42nd

The first British immigrants came to **Maryland** in 1634. In 1649, their governor drew up a law that enforced religious tolerance, and many people came to Maryland to worship freely. The colony adopted its first constitution in 1776. Maryland refused to become a state until colonies claiming land in the west that was not part of their official boundaries gave up that land. Their demands were met in 1781, and Maryland became the seventh state in 1788.

 Statehood Year: 1788
The 7th state
Coin Issue Year: 2000

MINNESOTA
1858

WISCONSIN
1848

MICHIGAN
1837

MAINE
1820

NEW HAMPSHIRE
1788

VERMONT
1791

MASSACHUSETTS
1788

NEW YORK
1788

RHODE ISLAND
1790

CONNECTICUT
1788

IOWA
1846

PENNSYLVANIA
1787

NEW JERSEY
1787

ILLINOIS
1818

INDIANA
1816

OHIO
1803

DELAWARE
1787

MARYLAND
1788

WEST
VIRGINIA
1863

VIRGINIA
1788

MISSOURI
1821

KENTUCKY
1792

NORTH CAROLINA
1789

TENNESSEE
1796

SOUTH
CAROLINA
1788

ARKANSAS
1836

ALABAMA
1819

GEORGIA
1788

MISSISSIPPI
1817

LOUISIANA
1812

FLORIDA
1845

Massachusetts
"The Bay State"

Capital
Boston

State Bird
Chickadee

State Flower
Mayflower

Land Area
7,838 sq. mi.
(20,300 sq. km)

State Tree
American elm

Rank in Size
45th

The first Pilgrims landed in **Massachusetts** in 1620 and established a colony. They named it Plymouth, after the town they sailed from in England. In 1629, a religious group called the Puritans were given permission to leave England to settle and govern the Massachusetts Bay Colony. By 1640, at least 10,000 people had settled there. In 1691, the Plymouth Colony joined with the Massachusetts Bay Colony. In 1780, Massachusetts drew up its constitution, and the colony became a state in 1788.

 Statehood Year: 1788
The 6th state
Coin Issue Year: 2000

Michigan
"The Wolverine State"

Capital
Lansing

State Bird
Robin

State Flower
Apple blossom

Land Area
56,809 sq. mi.
(147,136 sq. km)

State Tree
White pine

Rank in Size
22nd

Michigan was first explored by the French. By 1700, France had established forts and trading posts in the Michigan region. After the French and Indian War, the French left the area and the British moved in. But in the following years, many British settlers were killed by Indians. In 1774, the British gave the land to Quebec. After the Revolutionary War, the United States gained control of Michigan. The region became part of the Northwest Territory and was admitted to statehood in 1837.

 Statehood Year: 1837
The 26th state
Coin Issue Year: 2004

Minnesota
"The Gopher State"

Capital
St. Paul

State Bird
Common loon

State Flower
Pink and white
lady slipper

Land Area
79,617 sq. mi.
(206,207 sq. km)

State Tree
Norway pine

Rank in Size
14th

Fur traders were some of the earliest people to explore **Minnesota**. The first fur traders to set foot in Minnesota were French. In 1763, after the French and Indian War, Great Britain claimed land that included most of Minnesota. After the Revolutionary War, the British gave the land to the United States. The British still hunted and trapped furs there until after the War of 1812. In 1849, Congress established the Minnesota Territory, and Minnesota became a state in 1858.

Statehood Year: 1858
The 32nd state
Coin Issue Year: 2005

Mississippi
"The Magnolia State"

Capital
Jackson

State Bird
Mockingbird

State Flower
Magnolia

Land Area
46,914 sq. mi.
(121,506 sq. km)

State Tree
Magnolia

Rank in Size
31st

Congress established the **Mississippi** Territory in 1798. The territory was considered valuable because ownership of it allowed access to the Mississippi River and the port of New Orleans. In the late 1700s and early 1800s, Native Americans controlled much of the Mississippi region. Mississippi became a state in 1817. By 1832, most of the Native Americans who lived there had been forced to move into Indian Territory (what is now Oklahoma). As a result, many settlers came to Mississippi to set up farms.

Statehood Year: 1817
The 20th state
Coin Issue Year: 2002

Missouri
"The Show Me State"

Capital
Jefferson City

State Bird
Bluebird

State Flower
Hawthorn

Land Area
68,898 sq. mi.
(178,446 sq. km)

State Tree
Flowering
dogwood

Rank in Size
18th

In 1762, France gave Spain the region west of the Mississippi River. **Missouri** was a part of that region. Spain encouraged settlement in the territory. Napoleon Bonaparte, the ruler of France, forced Spain to turn the region back over to France in 1800. Three years later, France sold the Louisiana Territory, which included present-day Missouri, to the United States. In 1812, Congress established the Missouri Territory. Missouri became a state in 1821. At that time it was the westernmost border of the United States.

 Statehood Year: 1821
The 24th state
Coin Issue Year: 2003

Montana
"The Treasure State"

Capital
Helena

State Bird
Western
meadowlark

State Flower
Bitterroot

Land Area
145,556 sq. mi.
(376,991 sq. km)

State Tree
Ponderosa pine

Rank in Size
4th

The United States acquired **Montana** from France in the Louisiana Purchase. In 1805, President Thomas Jefferson sent Meriwether Lewis and William Clark to explore Montana and other western regions. The population of Montana grew when gold was discovered there in 1862. In 1876, Lieutenant Colonel George Custer's regiment and the Sioux and Cheyenne tribes fought a famous battle near the Little Bighorn River. More than 200 of Custer's men were killed. In 1889, Montana became a state.

 Statehood Year: 1889
The 41st state
Coin Issue Year: 2007

Nebraska
"The Cornhusker State"

Capital
Lincoln

State Flower
Goldenrod

State Tree
Cottonwood

State Bird
Western
meadowlark

Land Area
76,878 sq. mi.
(199,113 sq. km)

Rank in Size
15th

In 1854, Congress passed the Kansas-Nebraska Act, creating the territories of Kansas and **Nebraska**. By 1860, more than 28,000 people had settled in the Nebraska Territory. In 1862, Congress passed the Homestead Act. The Homestead Act gave free land to settlers in Nebraska and other western regions. As a result, thousands of people came to Nebraska. Many of the settlers became farmers. In 1867, Nebraska became a state.

 Statehood Year: 1867
The 37th state
Coin Issue Year: 2006

Nevada
"The Silver State"

Capital
Carson City

State Flower
Sagebrush

State Tree
Bristlecone pine
and the Single-leaf
piñon

State Bird
Mountain bluebird

Land Area
109,806 sq. mi.
(284,396 sq. km)

Rank in Size
7th

Mexico gave the United States **Nevada** and other nearby lands in 1848. In 1849, Nevada, along with Utah and parts of other present-day states, became the State of Deseret after being settled by Joseph Smith and the Mormons. After silver was discovered in 1859, thousands of people came from the East to Nevada. They settled in a town they called Virginia City. As a result of this population growth, President Buchanan made Nevada a territory in 1861. Soon after, in 1864, Nevada became a state.

 Statehood Year: 1864
The 36th state
Coin Issue Year: 2006

New Hampshire
"The Granite State"

Capital
Concord

State Bird
Purple finch

State Flower
Purple lilac

Land Area
8,969 sq. mi.
(23,231 sq. km)

State Tree
White birch

Rank in Size
44th

New Hampshire was first settled in 1623, three years after the Pilgrims landed at Plymouth Rock in Massachusetts. Several battles of the French and Indian War took place on New Hampshire soil from 1689 to 1763. In December of 1774, a group of New Hampshire colonists took over a British fort, which helped spark the Revolutionary War. In 1776, New Hampshire created its own constitution, making it the first colony to claim its independence from Britain. The colony became a state in 1788.

 Statehood Year: 1788
The 9th state
Coin Issue Year: 2000

New Jersey
"The Garden State"

Capital
Trenton

State Bird
Eastern goldfinch

State Flower
Purple violet

Land Area
7,419 sq. mi.
(19,215 sq. km)

State Tree
Red oak

Rank in Size
46th

New Jersey was first settled by the Dutch and the Swedes in the early 1600s. In 1664, Great Britain won control of New Jersey. Before the Revolutionary War, the British began making laws that many colonists thought were unfair. One of the laws forced the colonists to pay a tax on British goods. Some residents of New Jersey protested the tax by holding a tea party similar to the more famous Boston Tea Party. They snuck on board British ships and burned boxes of tea. In 1776, New Jersey declared its independence from Britain. It became a state in 1787.

 Statehood Year: 1787
The 3rd state
Coin Issue Year: 1999

New Mexico
"The Land of Enchantment"

Capital
Santa Fe

State Bird
Roadrunner

State Flower
Yucca

Land Area
121,365 sq. mi.
(314,334 sq. km)

State Tree
Piñon pine

Rank in Size
5th

The Spanish set up a colony in **New Mexico** in 1598. They forced the local Indians to work for them, and the Indians fought back in 1680. They pushed the Spanish out of their land for a while, but in 1692, the Spanish took over again. This time, the Spanish and the Indians got along peacefully. New Mexico became part of Mexico in 1821, but its residents often rebelled against Mexican rule. With the help of forces from the United States, they won independence from Mexico. The colony became a territory in 1850 and a state in 1912.

 Statehood Year: 1912
The 47th state
Coin Issue Year: 2008

New York
"The Empire State"

Capital
Albany

State Bird
Bluebird

State Flower
Rose

Land Area
47,224 sq. mi.
(122,310 sq. km)

State Tree
Sugar maple

Rank in Size
30th

The territory now known as **New York** was originally called New Netherland, because its first settlers were from the Netherlands. Present-day New York City was named New Amsterdam after the Netherlands' capital city. England took over New Netherland in 1664 and renamed it New York, after the Duke of York. But as a result of the Revolutionary War, New York won its independence from England. New York City was the nation's capital from 1785 to 1790. George Washington took the oath of office there in 1789 to become the nation's first president. In 1788, New York became a state.

 Statehood Year: 1788
The 11th state
Coin Issue Year: 2001

North Carolina
"The Tar Heel State"

Capital
Raleigh

State Bird
Cardinal

State Flower
Flowering
dogwood

Land Area
48,718 sq. mi.
(126,180 sq. km)

State Tree
Pine

Rank in Size
29th

In 1585, the English established a colony on **North Carolina's** Roanoke Island. Their governor went back to England to get supplies and returned in 1590 to find that the colony was deserted. No one knows what happened to the people who lived there. The English did not come back to settle in the area permanently until about 1650. But settlement was difficult because the colonists had to fight Indians, and pirates sailed along the shores. North Carolina became one of the original 13 states in 1789.

North Dakota
"The Peace Garden State"

Capital
Bismarck

State Bird
Western
meadowlark

State Flower
Wild prairie rose

State Tree
American elm

Land Area
68,994 sq. mi.
(178,695 sq. km)

Rank in Size
17th

Lewis and Clark passed through **North Dakota** during their expedition to the Pacific Ocean. In the 1800s, western settlement was slowed by the Sioux, who protested the takeover of their land. The Dakota Territory was established in 1861, and the territory was opened to homesteaders. Also in 1881, Sitting Bull, a famous Sioux leader, surrendered to the United States, assuring peace in the region. This allowed many people from the East to settle in North Dakota. In 1889, North Dakota became a state.

 Statehood Year: 1789
The 12th state
Coin Issue Year: 2001

 Statehood Year: 1889
The 39th state
Coin Issue Year: 2006

Ohio
"The Buckeye State"

Capital
Columbus

State Flower
Scarlet carnation

State Tree
Buckeye

State Bird
Cardinal

Land Area
40,953 sq. mi.
(106,067 sq. km)

Rank in Size
35th

Ohio became part of the Northwest Territory in 1787. Several Indian tribes fought against the settlers who came to the territory. In 1795, peace was achieved through the Treaty of Greenville, signed by Indian leaders and settlers. With the treaty, the Indians gave two-thirds of the Ohio region to the United States. After this treaty was signed, many more settlers came to Ohio. In 1803, Ohio became a state.

 Statehood Year: 1803
The 17th state
Coin Issue Year: 2002

Oklahoma
"The Sooner State"

Capital
Oklahoma City

State Flower
Mistletoe

State Tree
Redbud

State Bird
Scissor-tailed flycatcher

Land Area
68,679 sq. mi.
(177,877 sq. km)

Rank in Size
19th

For hundreds of years, Cheyenne, Comanche, Pawnee, Wichita, and other Native American tribes roamed the plains and hunted for buffalo on the sprawling grasslands in the region we know as **Oklahoma**. But in the 1800s, the United States government bought up their land and forced the Indians onto reservations. On April 22, 1889, central Oklahoma was opened for settlement. About 50,000 people had moved in by that evening. In 1890, the United States created the Territory of Oklahoma, and in 1907, Oklahoma became a state.

Statehood Year: 1907
The 46th state
Coin Issue Year: 2008

Oregon
"The Beaver State"

Capital
Salem

State Flower
Oregon grape

State Tree
Douglas fir

State Bird
Western meadowlark

Land Area
96,003 sq. mi.
(248,646 sq. km)

Rank in Size
10th

Fur trading was very important in the early history of **Oregon**. In the 1800s, many American and British fur trading companies opened in Oregon. John McLoughlin, the British director of the Hudson's Bay Company, ruled the Oregon region for about 20 years and helped many people settle the land. He is known as the father of Oregon. Later, more people from the East traveled along the Oregon Trail to settle in Oregon. In 1848, Oregon became a territory. It achieved statehood in 1859.

 Statehood Year: 1859
The 33rd state
Coin Issue Year: 2005

Pennsylvania
"The Keystone State"

Capital
Harrisburg

State Flower
Mountain laurel

State Tree
Hemlock

State Bird
Ruffed grouse

Land Area
44,820 sq. mi.
(116,083 sq. km)

Rank in Size
32nd

Pennsylvania was settled by Swedish and Dutch immigrants in the mid-1600s. In 1664, the English captured the region, who soon gave the land to William Penn as payment for a debt owed to Penn's father. He came to Pennsylvania (which means "Penn's Woods") in 1682 with fellow Quakers and governed the land. His family governed Pennsylvania until the start of the Revolutionary War in 1775. The city of Philadelphia was the nation's capital from 1790 to 1800. It was here that the Continental Congress adopted the Declaration of Independence in 1776 and the Constitutional Convention adopted the United States Constitution in 1787.

 Statehood Year: 1787
The 2nd state
Coin Issue Year: 1999

Rhode Island

"The Ocean State"

Capital
Providence

State Flower
Violet

State Tree
Red maple

State Bird
Rhode Island Red

Land Area
1,045 sq. mi.
(2,707 sq. km)

Rank in Size
50th

Roger Williams established the first English settlement in **Rhode Island** in 1636. He was followed by others looking for religious freedom. Rhode Island was a prosperous region. Its location on the ocean made its city of Newport a busy port. In 1774, Rhode Island became the first colony to stop the importation of slaves by prohibiting slave trade. Rhode Islanders were also among the first to rebel against British authority. In 1769, they burned the British ship Liberty, which was docked at Newport. Another first occurred on May 4, 1776, when Rhode Island became the first of the 13 original colonies to declare its independence from Britain.

 Statehood Year: 1790
The 13th state
Coin Issue Year: 2001

South Carolina

"The Palmetto State"

Capital
Columbia

State Flower
Carolina jessamine

State Tree
Palmetto

State Bird
Carolina wren

Land Area
30,111 sq. mi.
(77,988 sq. km)

Rank in Size
40th

South Carolina was settled by the British in 1670. The area was a British colony, but the king allowed the settlers to rule themselves. He did so because he considered the South Carolina coast important in the colony's defense against French and Spanish invaders, and he wanted it to remain a British stronghold. In 1788, South Carolina became a state. But in 1860, the state was the first state to secede from the Union to protest Lincoln's move to end slavery. South Carolina was readmitted to the Union in 1868, after the Civil War.

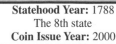
Statehood Year: 1788
The 8th state
Coin Issue Year: 2000

South Dakota
"The Mount Rushmore State"

Capital
Pierre

State Flower
Pasque

State Tree
Black Hills spruce

State Bird
Ring-necked pheasant

Land Area
75,896 sq. mi.
(196,571 sq. km)

Rank in Size
16th

South Dakota was settled by fur traders in the early 1800s. In 1861, Congress created the Dakota Territory, which included present-day South Dakota and North Dakota. In 1874, Lieutenant Colonel George Custer was sent by the United States government to the Black Hills to find out whether rumors of gold in the hills were true. Custer and his men did find gold, and a gold rush began. More gold was found in 1876, and more prospectors rushed to join the search. As the region's population grew, its residents pushed for statehood. In 1889, South Dakota became a state.

 Statehood Year: 1889
The 40th state
Coin Issue Year: 2006

Tennessee
"The Volunteer State"

Capital
Nashville

State Flower
Iris

State Tree
Tulip poplar

State Bird
Mockingbird

Land Area
41,220 sq. mi.
(106,759 sq. km)

Rank in Size
34th

Settlers lived in **Tennessee** in the 1760s, but the mountains in the region separated them from the other colonies. In the 1770s, Daniel Boone was hired to blaze a trail from Virginia through the mountains of Tennessee. This trail became known as the Wilderness Road. After its construction, more people were able to settle in Tennessee. The Chickasaw and Cherokee tribes also occupied much of the region, but Tennessee became a state in 1796. In 1818, the Chickasaw sold most of the land to the United States government. The Chickasaw remained, but were later forced to leave.

 Statehood Year: 1796
The 16th state
Coin Issue Year: 2002

Texas
"The Lone Star State"

Capital
Austin

State Flower
Bluebonnet

State Tree
Pecan

State Bird
Mockingbird

Land Area
261,914 sq. mi.
(678,358 sq. km)

Rank in Size
2nd

Texas was once a part of Mexico. But many Texans wanted their freedom, so they started the Texas Revolution in 1835. The most famous battle between Texas and Mexico took place in 1836 at the Alamo, a Spanish mission in San Antonio. There, 189 Texans fought thousands of Mexican soldiers. The fighting lasted 13 days, but the Mexican Army eventually won. The famous frontiersmen Davy Crockett and Jim Bowie fought and died at the Alamo. Texas fought back a month later and gained its independence from Mexico. After becoming a state in 1845, Texas left the Union in 1861 to join the Confederacy. The state was readmitted to the Union in 1870.

 Statehood Year: 1845
The 28th state
Coin Issue Year: 2004

Utah
"The Beehive State"

Capital
Salt Lake City

State Flower
Sego lily

State Tree
Blue spruce

State Bird
Seagull

Land Area
82,168 sq. mi.
(212,816 sq. km)

Rank in Size
12th

In 1847 the Mormons, a religious group led by Brigham Young, arrived in **Utah** and started the area's first major settlement. For several years the region was almost exclusively Mormon. In 1850, Congress created the Utah Territory, with Brigham Young as its governor. Many people in Utah wanted statehood, but Congress was concerned that the Mormon church was too involved in the area's government. After the Mormon church agreed to lessen its control on the territory, Utah became a state in 1896.

 Statehood Year: 1896
The 45th state
Coin Issue Year: 2007

Vermont
"The Green Mountain State"

Capital
Montpelier

State Flower
Red clover

State Tree
Sugar maple

State Bird
Hermit thrush

Land Area
9,249 sq. mi.
(23,956 sq. km)

Rank in Size
43rd

In the 1770s, the "Green Mountain Boys," a military force made up of men from **Vermont**, banded together to drive out settlers from New York, who laid claim to some of the land in Vermont. Some famous members of the group were Benedict Arnold and Ethan Allen. The Green Mountain Boys also fought and won some important battles in the Revolutionary War, including the capture of the British Fort Ticonderoga in 1775. In 1777, Vermont declared that it was an independent republic, called New Connecticut. It remained an independent republic until 1791, when it became a state.

 Statehood Year: 1791
The 14th state
Coin Issue Year: 2001

Virginia
"Old Dominion"

Capital
Richmond

State Flower
American dogwood

State Tree
American dogwood

State Bird
Cardinal

Land Area
39,598 sq. mi.
(102,558 sq. km)

Rank in Size
37th

The first permanent English settlement in the colonies was in **Virginia's** Jamestown, settled in 1607. In 1619, it was the site of the meeting of America's first legislative assembly. But the settlement suffered many setbacks. In 1622 and 1644, Indians attacked Jamestown and killed hundreds of its residents. Virginia became a royal colony in 1624, governed by leaders sent from England. In 1788, Virginia became a state. One year later, George Washington, a Virginian, was elected as the first President of the United States. Three of the next four Presidents were also from Virginia.

 Statehood Year: 1788
The 10th state
Coin Issue Year: 2000

Washington
"The Evergreen State"

Capital
Olympia

State Bird
Willow goldfinch

State Flower
Coast rhododendron

Land Area
66,581 sq. mi.
(172,445 sq. km)

State Tree
Western hemlock

Rank in Size
20th

Washington was settled by British and American traders. In 1818, the two countries signed a treaty that allowed them to trade and settle in the region. But even after the treaty, the countries could not agree on the boundary. In 1846, President Polk signed another treaty with Great Britain. In this treaty, the two countries came to an agreement. The region that is now the state of Washington went to America, while the British kept Vancouver Island. In 1883, railroad lines were completed that linked Washington with the Eastern United States. Washington became a state in 1889.

 Statehood Year: 1889
The 42nd state
Coin Issue Year: 2007

West Virginia
"The Mountain State"

Capital
Charleston

State Bird
Cardinal

State Flower
Rhododendron

Land Area
24,087 sq. mi.
(62,384 sq. km)

State Tree
Sugar maple

Rank in Size
41st

West Virginia was once part of the Virginia Colony. Early on, the western part of the colony demanded its own government. In the mid-1800s the region became even more divided over the slavery debate. Eastern Virginia had many large plantations with hundreds of slaves. The plantation owners controlled the government, and the westerners felt they were not fairly represented. When the Civil War began in 1861, the western region declared its independence from Virginia and joined the side of the Union states. Two years later, West Virginia became a state.

 Statehood Year: 1863
The 35th state
Coin Issue Year: 2005

Wisconsin
"The Badger State"

Capital	**State Bird**
Madison	Robin
State Flower	**Land Area**
Wood violet	54,314 sq. mi.
	(140,672 sq. km)
State Tree	
Sugar maple	**Rank in Size**
	25th

The first European to see **Wisconsin** was Frenchman Jean Nicolet. Searching for a water route to China, he sailed from Quebec to what is now called Green Bay. When he landed on the shore in 1634, he expected to be greeted by Chinese officials. Instead, he met Winnebago Indians. Disappointed, Nicolet returned to Quebec and told people there that America was even larger than they thought. Wisconsin became a territory of the United States in 1836 and achieved statehood in 1848.

 Statehood Year: 1848
The 30th state
Coin Issue Year: 2004

Wyoming
"The Equality State"

Capital	**State Bird**
Cheyenne	Meadowlark
State Flower	**Land Area**
Indian paintbrush	97,105 sq. mi.
	(251,501 sq. km)
State Tree	
Cottonwood	**Rank in Size**
	9th

In the 1800s three important trails went through **Wyoming**: the California Trail, the Mormon Trail, and the Oregon Trail. Pioneers from the East followed these trails through the South Pass, which wound through the Rocky Mountains. In 1846, Congress voted to build forts along the Oregon Trail to protect pioneers from Indian attacks. The Territory of Wyoming was organized in 1868. Wyoming became a state in 1890.

 Statehood Year: 1890
The 44th state
Coin Issue Year: 2007